THE ENGLISH DICTIONARY

EVASION —
THE ENGLISH DICTIONARY

EVASION —
THE ENGLISH DICTIONARY
∧

MAGGIE BALISTRERI

MELVILLE HOUSE PUBLISHING
HOBOKEN, NEW JERSEY

PARTS OF THIS BOOK HAVE APPEARED ON THE VOCABULA REVIEW
(VOCABULA.COM) AND THESCREAMONLINE.COM. *LIKE* WAS BROADCAST
ON WNYC RADIO.

MELVILLE HOUSE PUBLISHING
P.O. BOX 3278
HOBOKEN, NJ 07030

BOOK DESIGN: DAVID KONOPKA

ISBN: 0-9718659-7-3
THIRD PRINTING | DECEMBER 2003

LIBRARY OF CONGRESS CATALOGING-IN-PUBLICATION DATA

BALISTRERI, MAGGIE, 1971-
    THE EVASION-ENGLISH DICTIONARY / MAGGIE BALISTRERI.-- 1ST ED.
        P. CM.
    ISBN 0-9718659-7-3
    1. ENGLISH LANGUAGE--EUPHEMISM--DICTIONARIES. I. TITLE.
    PE1449.B315 2003
    423'.1--DC21
                                                        2003011659

The true use of speech is not to express our wants as to conceal them.

— Oliver Goldsmith

So it remains to microanalysts of interaction to lumber in where the self-respecting decline to tread. A question of pinning with our ten thumbs what ought to be secured with a needle.

— Erving Goffman

This is a short book about short words—*like* and *but*, *it* and *you*—the mainstays of speech that go unexamined, those throw-away words by which we reveal what we mean, no matter how hard we try not to.

This is a dictionary, in other words, to help you translate not only somebody else's speech but your own, from evasion to English, trick to truth. It identifies and interprets shibboleths of shamming, words we use either out of slackness of speech or because they get us what we want. Either way, whether daft or deft, we use these words to duck the truth.

So, here are some problematic terms and suggested substitutions. Most of the words in *The Evasion-English Dictionary* earned inclusion because hearing them annoyed me. But some entries were born on occasions when I found myself struck by the absence of evasion in someone's speech.

Change your words, I believe, and you change your deeds. It is, for example, harder to look somebody in the eye and say "I am unproductive" than it is to say "I feel unproductive." We do what is easy, and if I cringe at the admission that I am unproductive, perhaps that will spur me to industry. If I commit to being honest, I'll have less to evade.

The hope, in other words, is that this taxonomy of speech will inject a little self-consciousness into our daily speech. I don't know when *self-consciousness* became a negative term; maybe about the time that *consciousness* did. But let's put down the script and exert ourselves to be more honest. Discomfit yourself with the truth. Conversations should invite frankness. Instead, modern conversation is excruciatingly considerate; so determined are we to dodge discussion and the perils of disagreement that we dilute talk with unassailable phrases that do little more than lob back the ball to keep the game going.

Imagine if someone said, "I have money trouble but I don't like to think about it," and you replied, "If you don't think about it, you'll continue to have money trouble." The impertinence. The person will look askance as though to say, "No, dear, you've gone off script; the way it works is, *I* say, 'I have money trouble but I don't like to think about it,' and *you* say, 'There, there, hon.'"

It's as though we've turned the game of conversation into a ritual. A game, as Claude Lévi-Straus says in *The Savage Mind,* has any number of outcomes. You might lose. Or worse, you might win. A ritual, on the other hand, is the reenactment of the preferred instance of the game. No surprises. Such reenactment typically has come to make use of a number of meaningless placeholders, or *phatic communion,* to use the term coined by social anthropologist Bronislaw Malinowski, to describe phrases such as "Nice weather we're having," or "How ya doing" (the latter, by the way, not insignificantly lacking a question mark). For instance, I recently watched two people pass each other in the office. One greeted the other with, "Hey, how's it going." The second person, whose first language isn't English, stopped, thought for a moment, and began to answer the question sincerely: "Well, not so great...." Too late; Guy 1 was already past us and around the corner. Guy 2 looked at me bewildered. "Why did he ask if he didn't want the answer?"

We use phatic communion to establish sociability; it is civility clearing its throat. Ideally, this form of speech leads up to more substantive discussion. Unfortunately, as the two guys show, it often doesn't work that way, and phatic communion has stretched to comprise much of common discourse. It protracts throughout the conversation, a preface to empty discourse—a ritualized game.

The suggestion of the *E.E.D.*, then, is that you risk losing. Risk winning. Stretch your muscles. No more placeholders, no more *phatic communion*. Say what you mean, however discomfiting, to you or your listener. Purge from your speech that Creole of English, that pop-culture patois, that American dodge of a dialect I call Evasion-English.

THE EVASION-ENGLISH DICTIONARY

because = so
Effect turns out to be cause.

I read in a newspaper article a few years ago that Cardinal John O'Connor was grumbling because Little League and soccer games were "sometimes scheduled on Sunday mornings—and that, in too many cases, they are causing religion to be pushed aside." *Causing* religion to be pushed aside? Maybe *exposing* that religion has been pushed aside. It's always a buyer's market: It's not that kids are losing interest in church because soccer's set for Sunday. That's the tail wagging the dog. It's more that kids have lost interest in church, and that frees up their Sundays.

---

*I need to be around people all the time **because** I get bored easily.*

*Young men are drawn to violence **because** Hollywood glorifies it.*

*I push my kids to be open with me **because** they tend to be shy and withdrawn.*

*I don't write much anymore **because** I stay really late at the office.*

*I lack confidence **because** I don't get much positive feedback.*

because = so
(continued)

*I've always made it a point to be involved in her activities and encourage her every step of the way **because** she's extremely sensitive to my opinion.*

*I can't seem to focus on my work **because** all these other distractions keep coming up.*

*People don't value the teaching profession **because** teachers' salaries are so low.*

besides = mainly

Consequence is motive: When the speaker is ashamed of the truth.

When I hear the word *besides,* I think of not "alongside" or "next to," but instead I picture the "B" side, or the flip side of an LP. Too often, what follows the word *besides* in a narrative is usually the flip side in meaning or intention of what precedes it.

I was distraught when she broke up with me. I couldn't eat, I couldn't sleep; I didn't care about work or anything. But then I realized that I had to get on with my life.... Besides, there's this cute girl in my office I've always wanted to ask out.

She decided to accept the offer from the state university. It has the same course offerings, and she knows a few people who went there and loved it.... Besides, the other school was so expensive, not to mention clear across the country.

The job was supposed to start in two weeks, but I requested another week and a half. There are so many things I need to finish up here before I leave; I want things to be up-to-date for the next guy. I wanted to show some consideration for the company.... Besides, I need some time to catch my breath, just hang out. Once I start the new job, it'll be six months before I can take a vacation.

besides = mainly
(continued)

*No, we're still together. It's so hard to break up. I'm thinking I'll give it another few weeks. Who knows, you know?... **Besides**, my birthday's coming up soon, and it's gonna be hard enough to adjust; I don't want to deal with spending my birthday alone on top of that.*

*It wasn't easy to just leave my job, my boyfriend, everything, for this job, but I know that in the long run, I made the right decision.... **Besides**, I was getting tired of the relationship, and I couldn't seem to break up with him.*

*I know that Chris is gonna be there, but we're still friends with some of the same people, and this party will be one of the few times I'll get to see them.... **Besides**, I sort of like the idea of showing up with somebody new.*

but = because
When simultaneity of action
turns out to be cause and effect.

I heard somebody say, "I couldn't stop crying *but* I had a really good support system of friends who sat with me and listened without judging."

Aside from lamenting that the word *judge* has come to be a negative word, despite its denotation of weighing both sides of an issue (unless that is precisely what clouds its connotation), I've always been leery of the term *support system*. I imagine scaffolds hugging buildings, just waiting for the first fissure to crack the façade. *Support system* presupposes an inherent structural weakness. It's best to repair that weakness.

Instead there are support systems to stabilize you through every effort in life, support systems to help you quit one thing or start another; become this or stop being that. The only thing there isn't a support system for is an overreliance on support systems. Huddling around sharing a crying jag with others is an enticement to wallow in despair, a well-meaning invitation to tick off trauma trinkets with a bunch of strangers or hired listeners.

And in certain cases, the opportunity to express despair can create despair. A case of "invention is the mother of necessity": Consider a 1997 study in *The Lancet* revealing that in Lithuania, where personal injury insurance wasn't available until recently. Not only did drivers who were involved in rear-end collisions not report whiplash, but they weren't at all familiar with the term.

So, you couldn't stop crying *but* you had a really good support system of friends who sat around with you and listened without judging? Maybe you couldn't stop crying *because* you had a really good support system of friends who sat around with you and listened without judging.

but = because
(continued)

*Joey's test scores are down a little **but** we don't like to make a big deal about things like grades.*

*I'm not exactly rich **but** I like nice things.*

*We're broke **but** we don't let it get us down.*

*We fight all the time **but** we've decided not to give up working on the relationship.*

*I'm not doing very well at work **but** I don't care.*

*Science and math scores are at an all-time low **but** self-esteem in twelve- to fifteen-year-olds is at an all-time high.*

*They drive me crazy **but** my parents are very involved in my life.*

*She didn't complete the program **but** she feels good about herself regardless.*

*They're rich **but** they live modestly and they're really careful about their money.*

*I didn't finish reading the book **but** I think I've read enough to know what the author's getting at.*

but = because
(continued)

*I learned a lot in that class **but** it was really hard.*

*I've made a lot of mistakes in my life **but** my family's always there to back me up.*

*I fuck up a lot **but** I know she'll always forgive me.*

*She has a lot of valid points **but** she's so critical.*

*My students are having a tough time focusing **but** I encourage them every step of the way.*

*They're a challenging bunch of kids **but** I'm trying to convey my respect and admiration for them.*

*I've always wished that my daughter would become a ballerina **but** she seems to be more interested in sports.*

*I lose my temper sometimes **but** my family knows I love them.*

*Maybe she's successful **but** she doesn't have much of a social life.*

*My daughter loves sports **but** I have always wished that she would become a ballerina.*

but = because
(continued)

*The reading for the class is really hard **but** the way I approach it is to try to relate it to my own experiences.*

*It's getting worse **but** I'm not gonna think about it.*

*Women don't enjoy the same rights as men in this culture **but** we believe in the tradition and find ways to express ourselves in the home.*

Plutarch sent a letter of consolation to his wife after the death of their child that included a caution:

"...[W]hat is most grave and to be dreaded in such a case holds no terrors for me: 'the visits of pernicious women' and their cries and their chiming in with lamentations, whereby they polish and whet the keen edge of pain, and do not allow our grief to subside either from other influences or of itself.... For when people see the houses of their friends in flames, they put the fire out with all the speed or power at their command; but when those friends are themselves ablaze with fire in their hearts, they bring more fuel."

but = bu(llshi)t

The word *but* is the contraction of *bu(llshi)t*.

In college my teacher explained the writing workshop format: Somebody reads, and then the rest of the class offers critiques. "But," she said, "I ask that you all respect each other and start with something positive, a little reinforcement, before you offer a more direct criticism of the work."

Somebody asked, "But what if you don't have anything positive to say?"

"Well, you can find something."

"Like what? What if there's nothing?"

The teacher was exasperated at this point. "Find something."

"Well, tell me the kind of thing I could say. Like what?"

"You can praise the energy of the writing, or talk about what direction you think the writer is going and praise that.... But it should be genuine!"

For the rest of the semester, we honed hitting that tone of forced fawning before stating the criticism. In turn we learned to tune out the start of anybody's critique, since the heart of it followed the perfunctory praise.

The word that signals this tonal change from obligatory preface to truth is *but*. Whenever I hear a particularly politic use of *but* following a compliment or empty words meant as reinforcement, I visualize certain extra letters buried in the *but*.

but = bu(llshi)t
(continued)

---

*I see your point... **bu(llshi)t** I think we should do it this way.*

*Well, I'm really glad you brought that to my attention. I want nothing more than for employees to feel that they can come to me with suggestions for improvement. After all, I consider this company to be a team. **Bu(llshi)t** I can't implement that kind of change at this point in time.*

*I'm married to a wonderful man, loving, witty, a doting father to our three children, **bu(llshi)t** lately I've wondered what it would be like to be single again, get a fresh start.*

*The letter was right there on her desk. I know I shouldn't have read it; I mean, trust is so important in a relationship, and I really believe that, **bu(llshi)t** I wanted to find out once and for all, so I did it, I read the letter.*

*It's not that I don't still love you, and I can't imagine living without you, **bu(llshi)t** I think we should break up.*

*I love being with you, and I wouldn't trade our time together for anything in the world, **bu(llshi)t** I just need this time alone.*

but = bu(llshi)t
(continued)

I know that's it's an indulgence and I can't really afford it, **bu(llshi)t** *I've always wanted it and so I just said "Fuck it" and went ahead and did it.*

He's a wonderful artist, a brilliant writer, **bu(llshi)t** *he's self-destructive and hasn't worked on his craft in ten years.*

It was a difficult decision, and believe me, I was heartbroken. Inconsolable, really; **bu(llshi)t** *I really wanted to move to a bigger place, so I had to find another home for my dog.*

We see the great insights in this work and wish you all the best in your future endeavors, **bu(llshi)t** *we feel it isn't quite right for our book list and have decided to pass on your book idea.*

buy into = own
You bought it. Now own it.

The phrase *buy into*, as in *they buy into the idea that...*, is a way
to gently criticize the belief a person holds without criticizing
the person. Hate the sin, love the sinner. For example, if I am
one of the lamentable masses who *buys into the idea* that material possessions are a sign of my self-worth, how exactly is that
different from the sentence "She's so shallow, she thinks her
self-worth is measured in material possessions"? Same belief,
but in the latter locution, the judgment is stronger. I like
stronger. Go ahead, judge. I'd rather be credited as owning a
thought than to be characterized as a dupe in some unnamed
trickster's machinations. Nobody sold me nothin'.

I find it most patronizing in the characterization of women
as chronic chumps who *buy into* the media's depiction of
female beauty this, society's standard of beauty that. You know
what? When I pored over glamour magazines as a teenager,
willing my hair to uncurl, it was because I was shallow. I flat-
ter myself to believe that eventually, I changed—magazine sub-
scriptions, for starters.

---

*Parents **buy into** this myth that their kids have to
attend the perfect preschool and have the right
extracurriculars on their records or else the Ivy
League schools will just pass them by.*

buy into = own
(continued)

Women **buy into** the idea that they have to be perfect and that beauty has to conform to magazine standards.

As a culture we **buy into** this pressure of keeping up with the Joneses by having a fancy house and taking lots of exotic trips.

Men **buy into** the old saw that a man's not supposed to cry.

The culture was in crisis and the people weren't informed. There were many factors that contributed to the hardships they experienced that made them **buy into** the promises made by a charismatic leader.

Uninformed voters **buy into** the idea that there are only two parties, when in fact....

People still **buy into** the idea that a family means a Mom, a Dad, and 2.3 kids.

What we see are kids who have no choice but to **buy into** the myth that if they don't conform, they won't be accepted.

buy into = own
(continued)

*They **buy into** the idea that if they're not accepted, why, it's a fate worse than death!*

*There's just an onslaught of media images telling you that this is the way you should be and so after a while, you can't help but **buy into** it.*

does = doesn't
Hindsight is 20/20? So is insight.

Does this dress make me look fat?

In the history of that question, only a fool has answered yes. Yes isn't an option. "Does this dress make me look fat" is not a yes-or-no question. It's a no-or-no question. Those are your options.

It's also a classic *does* question, setting up the listener to be not a yes-man but a no-man: "Nooo, that dress doesn't make you look fat. What? Fat? I can like, barely see you, you're so thin in that dress!"

I always feel glued to the floor when somebody hits me with a *does* question that turns out to be an end-run around the word *yes*. "Does this dress make me look fat" is the most trivial of the *does* questions, so go ahead, ask me the question, I'll tell you the lie. Reassuring you about your looks carries no down side.

But the stakes are higher when the *does* question comes in the form of "So I made one stupid mistake. *Does* that make me a bad person?" This question often elicits from the listener reassurance or sympathy about behavior that the listener might consider stupid or unwise or even appalling. The most unsettling *does* questions come up in our various arenas of confession. Talk shows—our monster markets—give occasion to people who unabashedly confess, apologize profusely, indulge in a good bawl, and then wrap it up neatly with the question, "One mistake! Does that make me a bad person?"

Any heartful person wants to check the impulse to say, "Yes, yes it does," and might prefer to keep silent, but silence isn't an option when you're buttonholed. The *does* question is faux-rhetorical; the speaker wants a hug, so the listener ends up lying instead of lying low.

does = doesn't
(continued)

---

*I thought I could entrust my children with him. He'd been so good with them. Am I a bad parent because I take some time for myself every once in a while? You know, I'm not old; I like to go out too, just like everybody else. **Does** that make me a bad person?*

*So I made one stupid mistake. I said I was sorry. Believe me; if I could take back the past twelve years, I would. I wasn't mature enough to handle the responsibility of a family, and I didn't have the brains to think about it beforehand. Things just got out of control. I just made one mistake. **Does** that make me a bad person?*

*Where I'm from, I can leave my baby in a baby carriage outside of restaurants and not think twice about it. I just didn't think it would be such a problem to do the same here. I didn't know. **Does** that make me a bad person?*

*I kept it in a safe place. The bullets were clear across the room. And I had told her so many times never to touch my gun. I made a mistake. I should have gotten rid of it when she started to crawl. I know that now. I feel terrible. I was trying to protect my family. **Does** that make me a bad person?*

does = doesn't
(continued)

*Look, I made a mistake. I was sure I could make it
home if I just went slowly. I admit, I wasn't thinking
of the other people on the road. I guess I wasn't
thinking at all. But **does** that make me a bad person?*

*In my whole life, nothing like this has ever hap-
pened to me. I've never hurt anyone, ever. This was-
n't me; I mean, I did it, but it wasn't me. I am not a
murderer. I let my emotions get the better of me that
one time. Now, **does** that make me a bad person?*

"If you don't consider what happened in Oklahoma, Tim is a good
person."

—Michael Fortier, former Army pal of Timothy McVeigh,
at the Oklahoma City bombing trial

even though = because
The downside is the upside.

Everything is present from the start. The regrets we have in retrospect sometimes turn out to have been motivators. *Even though* is perhaps the weakest of the evasions, the one people are most likely to see through. For example, when fourteen-year-olds dye their hair green *even though* it'll piss off their parents, most parents understand that that's the whole point.

---

*I had a fling **even though** I knew she'd break up with me if she ever found out. It's okay. I guess I was thinking about leaving the relationship anyway.*

***Even though** I had a lot of responsibilities, I decided to quit my job and look for something else. At least I don't have to deal with that place anymore.*

*Having roommates is great **even though** it means I'm never alone.*

*He brought up the same old argument right there at the party **even though** he knew it would upset me.*

***Even though** she was married, and there was no chance she was going to leave her husband for me, we fell in love.*

even though = because
(continued)

I took the offer **even though** it would require a lot of time away from my family. I couldn't turn it down.

Even though it meant we would see less of each other, we decided that her going back to school was a good thing. Great, really.

I just had to stop at the store and exchange the shirt, **even though** it meant being late for the meeting and keeping my co-workers waiting.

I decided to change majors **even though** it means I'll be here another semester. Hey, what's another semester? Anyway, I kind of like it here.

She does it **even though** she knows it affects her health.

She just took off and was gone for hours **even though** she knew that I'd be worried wondering where she went.

Even though this doesn't involve me, I feel I can give you some sound advice.

I think I'm falling in love with him **even though** he'll be leaving town in a few months.

even though = because
(continued)

We decided to give this relationship a try **even though** he lives in California and I live in New York.

Even though it's a little risky, we did it.

Even though it meant possibly breaking up, I told her about the affair. I felt it was the right thing to do.

We decided to have a baby **even though** it meant Bob and I would have less time for each other.

Even though she knew it was mean, she went ahead and did it.

"Regret is not subsequent to the action, but present from the start."

—Alfred Adler

feel = am
It isn't feeling, it's fact.

These days, saying "You insulted me" is deemed by many to be too threatening. Saying instead "I feel insulted when you..." is the advice of self-help gurus, shrinks, and sensitivity trainers. This clunky sentence construction, called the "I statement," is supposed to help the speaker "own" her feelings and help the listener not become defensive.

Let's try it: I feel patronized when people couch their statements in terms of "I feel" instead of saying outright what is implied.

Who hears "I feel insulted when you..." and doesn't translate that as "You insulted me when you..."? Besides, talking about how you feel is a popular way to circumvent debate, since feelings are incontrovertible: "I can't help it, that's how I feel."

And so *feel* is the feel-good word. But I feel all this feeling has left us unfeeling. Rather than making us more sensitive, overusing this word has dulled us to feelings, specifically, the feelings of others. So trained are we to assess our own feelings at every turn that our speech rarely moves beyond them.

It's the height of audacity then, that after doing something wrong—presumably to somebody else—I could be so self-absorbed as to forgo attending to the other person's feelings and instead remain focused on myself: "I can't believe I did that. I *feel* so guilty!" Perhaps the self-absorption I betray in wanting to talk about my feelings after I've hurt yours is the reason I blundered in the first place.

feel = am
(continued)

---

*It was all my fault. I **feel** responsible.*

*I **feel** so guilty.*

*I **feel** so bad.*

*I can't believe I did that to you. I **feel** terrible.*

*Man, looks like you're doing all the work yourself. I **feel** so lazy and unproductive.*

*I can't believe I said that. I **feel** so mean.*

*I hate when I do that to him. I **feel** so disloyal.*

*I'm like a lot of people in my generation. I **feel** so apathetic about politics.*

*It's not so much what you said, but how you said it. I mean, you could tell me in a nicer way. This way, I **feel** so clueless.*

*I hate myself when I do that. I can hear myself saying it, and I think, 'Oh my God! I **feel** so fake.*

*I hate to be in that mental space. I **feel** so bitchy.*

hate = have

It's not grudging, it's begrudging.

In the middle of a conversation with an old friend I said "I hate to say it but..." when he interrupted with, "So don't."

The rascal. I had to wait a few minutes before contriving to *hate to say it* again.

Hardly anybody *hates to say it*; it's more that we hate to be known to have said it. Using the phrase *I hate to say* affects a coy unfamiliarity with the custom of criticism or snide comment. Implied is "I can't believe I'm saying this; it's so uncharacteristic of me." This elevates the speaker above those who are actually the kind of people who would say such things.

---

*I ended up not taking it. The apartment itself was great, lots of closet space, pretty nice-sized kitchen, but, I mean... well, I **hate** to say it's in a black neighborhood....*

*He was nice I guess. I **hate** to say he's not in my league....*

*No, that's great. Really. Good for you. I **hate** to say I had my heart set on it for myself....*

*I **hate** to say I'm holding out for something better....*

hate = have
(continued)

*The dress was nice enough. I mean, it's not that.
It's just, well, I **hate** to say she's fat....*

*I mean, what were you thinking? I **hate** to say you
had it coming....*

*She's a great co-worker, don't get me wrong, it's
just that she has a kid, so she's always, well, not
always but a lot of the time, she leaves early or
comes in late because of her kid, and, I **hate** to say
that I have to pick up her slack....*

*Did you see their house? I **hate** to say that ours is
bigger....*

*I was so jealous of his ex until I met her. I mean, I
hate to say I'm prettier....*

*I think it's a great idea, and I totally support her,
but I mean, asking me to pitch in; I don't know, I
hate to say, "What's in it for me," but....*

*I'm just saying, it could happen, and I **hate** to be
the one to say "I told you so."*

I know = even though
Admission is contrition.

An imposition is inexcusable. Unless, of course, you acknowledge it. Then it's okay. The sentence "I know, but hey, at least I admit it" is supposed to soften the blow since *at least* the speaker acknowledges it, *at least* the speaker recognizes that he or she is asking a lot of you—*at least*. The least we can do is often the most that we are willing to do.

---

*I was wondering if you could eyeball this for me. I have to turn it in this afternoon, and you're such a good editor. I hate to ask, **I know** you're busy.*

*I made us reservations for tonight at eight. **I know** it's short notice.*

*I invited them along. Yeah, **I know** you don't really like them.*

*I was wondering if you could add this to your list of things to do. No rush; **I know** it's not really your job. I can't believe I'm gonna go through with it. **I know** it's so mean.*

*I just don't feel like going. **I know** you had your heart set on it.*

I know = even though
(continued)

*I **know** this is the last thing you want to hear right now.*

*I **know** you hate it when I do that.*

*I'm gonna be letting a lot of people down. **I know** that sucks.*

*It's a little late to be asking for an extension, I **know** it's a lot to ask.*

*I lied. **I know**, I did.*

"He says, no varnish can hide the grain of the wood; and that the more varnish you put on, the more the grain will express itself."

—Charles Dickens, *Great Expectations*

the eye chart *it*

"Okay, please look at the eye chart. Is it clear?"

"Nope. Still blurry."

"How is it now?"

"It's getting better."

"How is it now?"

"It got blurrier. It was better the other way."

"How is it now?"

"Now it's good."

There's nothing wrong with the eye chart; *it* isn't blurry; *it* is just fine. What you mean when you say, "It's not clear" is that it isn't clear *to you*.

In other words, the aid to your deficiency isn't strong enough.

the house-proud *it* = I

A classic B-movie set-up is a perfect metaphor for the house-proud *it:* A babysitter receives a threatening phone call. "I'm going to kill you!" says a voice. She frantically calls the operator, and asks her to trace the call. Moments later the operator phones back the babysitter: "Listen to me. We've traced the call. It's coming from inside the house! Get out of the house! It's coming from inside!"

There are no externals. Despair, failure, success, happiness, all come from within: Within the individual, the family, the group.

It's coming from inside.

It felt small and cramped before we put in the mirrors.

It could use a makeover. A complete rehaul.

I had to do something about that corner; it was so empty and forlorn.

The décor just wasn't working for me; it didn't feel right.

I changed the living room around; it needed some life, character.

It was okay, but *it* wasn't what I wanted.

It still felt like *it* was missing something.

It was boring, conventional.

I was hoping you could tell me what *it* needed.

*The salesman explained that **it** was about form, not
function; **it** didn't need to actually do anything.*

"Though of a very ingenious mechanical turn, Nippers could never get
this table to suit him. He put chips under it, blocks of various sorts,
bits of pasteboard, and at last went so far as to attempt an exquisite
adjustment by final pieces of folded blotting paper. But no invention
would answer. If, for the sake of easing his back, he brought the table
lid at a sharp angle well up towards his chin, and wrote there like a
man using the steep roof of a Dutch house for his desk, then he
declared that it stopped the circulation in his arms. If now he lowered
the table to his waistbands and stooped over it in writing, then there
was a sore aching in his back. In short, the truth of the matter was,
Nippers knew not what he wanted. Or, if he wanted anything, it was
to be rid of a scrivener's table altogether."

—Herman Melville, *Bartleby the Scrivener*

the malefactory *it* = I
Agentless passives bemoan the
consequences of their own actions.

A criminal vaguely remembers holding his gun. Moments later
it "went off." "The situation" blew out of control. *It* got crazy,
and *it* all seemed to spiral out of control so fast.

---

*I did it. **It** was so stupid.*

***It** was wrong. I'm sorry.*

***It** was so mean-spirited. I know **it** hurt you.*

*I can't blame you for being angry. **It** was inconsid-
erate. I know, **it** was just wrong.*

***It** was chaotic and unstable. Definitely not a
healthy environment for a child.*

*I realize now how immature **it** was. I see that now.*

*You have to understand how crazy that time in my
life was. **It** was nuts.*

"I envy people who drink. At least they know what to blame everything on."

—Oscar Levant in the film *Humoresque*

The term *Cuvier's bone* refers to the demonstration by scientist Georges Leopard Cuvier (1769–1832) that from a single bone, a scientist can construct the entire animal. German philosopher Arthur Schopenhauer, in *Essays and Aphorisms*, extended this idea of the whole being contained in its parts:

"As a botanist can recognize the whole plant from one leaf, as Cuvier can construct the whole animal from one bone, so an accurate knowledge of man's character can be arrived at from a single characteristic action; and that is true even when this action involves some trifle—indeed this is often better for the purpose, for with important things people are on their guard, while with trifles they follow their own nature without much reflection."

Our culture's telling trifle, our Cuvier's bone, is the word *like,* from which the less sterling aspects of our character can be constructed. The word in its current use dates back to the 1950s—it appeared in William Gaddis's novel *The Recognitions* in 1955—but it was popularized by the 1980s' Valley Girl, and it still sounds just as dumb. But it's worse than mindless. This one little word happens to consistently trip our every mincing step toward clarity. You can ferret out *like* in most sloppy sentences. Look for *like*, and you'll track the roots of evasion: What follows is a taxonomy not only of *like* but also of the vexingly undercutting, vague, self-effacing, cowardly filler that passes for speech.

the undercutting *like*
Translation: I'm not smart; I'm cool. I don't
know where I picked up that knowledge.

---

*I think he meant it **like**, metaphorically.*

*You can't do that; it's **like**, a federal offense.*

*That was by **like**, Beethoven.*

*I just used the **like**, law of contrapositive to figure
out the answer.*

*Who? That guy? Oh, he's the ambassador to **like**,
Nigeria.*

*That's, **like**, an umlaut. Or something.*

*I think it's **like**, N-i-e-t-z, then, s-c-h-e, or something. I don't know.*

the vague *like*
Translation: Thereabouts.

---

*There were **like**, a thousand screaming fans.*

*Have you been outside? It's **like**, 100 degrees.*

*It was written **like**, two hundred years ago.*

*This was back in **like**, October.*

*How could I? I was **like**, twelve years old at the time.*

the self-effacing *like*
Translation: Virtue is shameful.

---

*No, I don't want to **like**, betray her trust.*

*Nah, I wanna try to **like**, do it myself.*

*I was **like**, school president and captain of the basketball team.*

*I want to try to be more, **like**, considerate.*

*I work out **like**, every day.*

*I volunteer for a few hours every week. I **like**, care about the environment and stuff.*

the cowardly *like*
Translation: I disagree. That is, if it's okay.

---

*I don't want to **like**, tell you what to do, but it just doesn't sound, **like**, nice.*

*I **like**, got a different answer for that question.*

*I think you're **like**, overreacting.*

*Are you sure? Didn't you say you were gonna **like**, pay me back later?*

*Did you **like**, misspell that?*

*I don't think you're **like**, being fair.*

the filler *like*
Translation: I finished my sentence.

*How could you do that? I mean, I went out of my way to meet you there, and then you didn't show, and you didn't even call, and it was **like**....*

*I've worked hard this past year, and I thought the company would recognize my work with a more substantial raise; I mean, this is less than the cost of living, and I have to think about my future, and, I mean, it's **like**....*

*Let's see if we can't work something out. I have to go to my supervisor to approve this raise, and she's gonna ask me what you've done for the company to distinguish yourself, and I'm gonna be **like**....*

the betrayer *like*
Translation: I lie.

---

*I was so upset I cried for **like**, three days.*

*We **like**, fell in love on the spot.*

*You bring up a good point, and I **like**, totally sympathize with you; however....*

*Oh, this is **like**, so not an imposition! No really, I **like**, want to do this for you.*

the apology *like*
Translation: Sorry, I'm inarticulate.

---

*I was **like**, wow.*

*He was **like**, "Oh my God!"*

*It was so interesting; it was **like**, I can't explain it.
You know what I mean?*

*I **like**, guess so.*

the multimedia *like*
Translation: Visual aid to follow.

Great movie. Amazing special effects. It was **like**.... (Strike a taken-aback facial expression.)

The baby was so cute. She was **like**.... (Look cute.)

I was so happy, I was **like**.... (Jump and clap hands.)

He said something sarcastic, and I was **like**.... (Glare.)

Then it went into all this technical jargon, and I was **like**.... (Look befuddled.)

Did you see what she wearing? I was **like**.... (Judge.)

staller *like*, part 1
Translation: Think, brain, think!

Man, this bag is heavy. What do you have in here,
like, a bowling ball?

Poetry? Yeah, me too. I love ***like***, Robert Frost.

You're from Belize? That's ***like***, south?

staller *like*, part 2
Translation: Uh, oh, math....

*Let's see, thirty percent off, so it's **like**, forty dollars.*

*Plus tip, double the tax; let's leave, **like**, sixty bucks?*

*Amortized over thirty years, that comes to **like**, a lot.*

oh, well

The passive-agressive never battles,
and never loses.

The passive-aggressive is a good enough actor to pretend to be a bad actor: "What's wrong? Oh... nothing...." In reality, this guilt-tripper is surefooted. His mock stoicism in the face of your insult is calculated to avoid confrontation yet end in his victory.

The word *confrontational* has a bad rap. It has come to connote a bully. In fact the word denotes a face-to-face, a meeting. I prefer confrontation to passive-aggression. A confrontation can be resolved, and it permits the confronted person an opportunity to dispute... which is the last thing a passive-aggressive wants.

Instead of being confrontational, the passive-aggressive lurks somewhere behind our ear and disappears before we can whirl around to face him.

The extended dance-track version of the passive-aggressive "oh, well" is "oh, well; what are you gonna do." That last bit isn't a rhetorical question: What are you gonna do? Because the onus is squarely on you.

You're going home? Good for you. Me? I have at least two more hours of work. **Oh, well**.

You pick first. It's not quite half, but **oh, well**.

Wow. That's a pretty good raise. You must be a better negotiator than I am. **Oh, well**.

oh, well
(continued)

You're right; you were here first. **Oh, well.**

Tomorrow? Oh. I was gonna take the day off. It's my birthday, but, **oh well.**

I guess today's not my lucky day. **Oh, well.**

I spent five hours on this paper. But if I have to rewrite it, I have to rewrite it. **Oh, well.**

No more seats? I guess I'm standing. **Oh, well.**

Oh, no, I asked for the dressing on the side. **Oh, well.** *No, that's okay; I'll eat it anyway.*

I wanted to be there for you. So I skipped the game; it was the playoffs, but **oh, well.**

No, you just go on ahead without me. I'll stay here and take care of the kids. You can tell me all about it when you get back. Sure sounds like a lot of fun. **Oh, well.**

I was hoping you'd come visit but if you're busy, you're busy. I'm not getting any younger. But **oh, well.** *What are you gonna do.*

the relationship
There is no third entity called
the relationship.

The most absurd character on the dating scene is The
Relationship Narrator. Maybe you have overheard this character in a restaurant, or worse, been on the receiving end of this
play-by-play:

> *Good, good; this is good. We're getting along! ... You
> know, communication is the cornerstone of every
> good relationship.... I think we're really clicking.
> This is going so well.... You're laughing at my
> jokes. You know, sharing a sense of humor is key....
> Um, just to step back for a moment, I feel really com-
> fortable with you. Not at all self-conscious.... I just
> have such a good feeling about this relationship.*

This superfluous narrating is the equivalent of subtitling a
movie—in the same language. It distracts from what it wants to
acknowledge. It's the same as asking me, "You liked that joke?"
while I'm laughing at it.

And what is every Relationship Narrator's favorite word?
*Relationship. Honey, let's talk about the relationship; I need to
talk about the relationship; I'm just trying to understand the
parameters of the relationship.* Talking about the relationship
by referring to it as The Relationship is a sure way to kill it. It
reminds me of a story about Duke Ellington. When he was told
of the newly coined term *bebop,* Ellington reportedly sighed,
and said, "Once you've named it, it's dead."

Another problem I have with saying *the relationship* is that
using the term makes it sound as though there is a third entity

the relationship
(continued)

called *the relationship*. It implies a cool distance from it—*it* being you and me—that I don't feel if I am genuinely in the relationship. I don't see it as "I plus you equals the relationship." Obviously $1 + 1 \neq 3$. In fact, I wouldn't even use $1 + 1 = 2$ as a model of the ideal mathematical representation of two people coming together because we lose the 1s; visually, neither part, neither 1, is preserved in the sum.

I'd rather imagine Roman numerals: $I + I = II$. It's closer to what two people look like together, and it's a lovely image as well. If I wanted to talk about the relationship, specifically problems in the relationship, I should use the word *you* or *me*. Those sturdy, side-by-side Roman numeral *I*s would serve as reminders.

the relationship = me

*I just feel you aren't putting as much energy and effort into **the relationship.***

*I feel I've invested enough of myself to deserve to know what you intend for **the relationship.***

*Are you even commited to **the relationship**? I can't tell.*

*You owe it to **the relationship**.*

*Your behavior lately is hurting **the relationship**.*

*I just don't think you take **the relationship** seriously.*

*It would mean a lot to me because it would be a sign that you value **the relationship**.*

the relationship = you

*Honey, we need to talk about **the relationship**.*

*I just don't feel like I'm getting what I want from **the relationship**.*

*Sometimes I think I put more into **the relationship** than I'm getting back.*

*I felt that **the relationship** held me back.*

*I have very clear ideas about what I'm looking for from **the relationship**.*

*There seem to be a lot of problems with the **relationship** and I don't feel you're making any effort to address them.*

***The relationship** needed a lot of work.*

*Even my friends can see that there are problems in **the relationship**.*

*There are certain things I think I'm perfectly justified in getting from **the relationship**.*

*In order for me to give myself up to **the relationship**, there are a lot of changes that need to be made.*

sensitive = insensitive

We express what we fail to contain.

There's a difference between *sensitive* and *emotional*. Sensitivity is what you take in; emotions are what you display. In the throes of an emotion, my ability to perceive, or be sensitive to, anything beyond that emotion is impaired.

Sometimes a person's great claims to sensitivity belie an inability or unwillingness to be sensitive. The outward affect of highly strung people suggests sensitivity—the gasps, the sighs, but mostly the reminder "I'm very sensitive"—but I wonder if the highly strung don't display sensitivity in proportion as they feel none. Think of a plant. A plant suggests the color green. We might say green as a defining characteristic of plants. In fact, the plant is green because out of all the colors in the spectrum, green is the only color that the plant cannot absorb. In other words, it exhibits what it can't possess.

*You know what? I can't even sit here listening to this. It's too sad. Let's talk about something else. You have to understand; I'm really **sensitive**.*

*I wanted to be there for you. But to see you suffer, every day, and not be able to help you—it was just too heartbreaking. I wasn't avoiding you, I was avoiding my feelings. You have to understand; I'm really **sensitive**.*

sensitive = insensitive
(continued)

I think that's so great that you volunteer. I couldn't do it; it would make me cry. You have to understand; I'm really **sensitive**.

I had to walk out of the movie. It was too sad. It would have just made me cry and cry and cry. You have to understand; I'm really **sensitive**.

I couldn't do that kind of work. It's too stressful. I just can't imagine seeing that kind of tragedy every day. You have to understand; I'm really **sensitive**.

It's hard, don't get me wrong. But I can't get involved in these kids' lives. It would break me apart, and then, what good would I be to them? You have to understand; I'm really **sensitive**.

It was literally making me sick. Every day, I'd go into the office and feel sick to my stomach. Can you blame me for quitting? You have to understand; I'm really **sensitive**.

I looked into that job too. It's so stressful, though; every day, you talk to people whose lives are so much worse than your own. I would feel so guilty and stressed out. I don't want to deal with that. You have to understand; I'm really **sensitive**.

should = won't

Pretension is nine-tenths of the lore.

School weaned us on partial credit. If we didn't get the answer right on a test, the teacher tossed us a few points for setting up the problem right, or for getting almost the right answer. Eh, good enough.

Even after graduation, we still try to get partial credit, especially in the area of self-improvement. If I don't quite do something that you think is commendable, at least I get some points for having thought about doing it.

That's where the word *should* comes in handy. *Should* buys time, postponing an action that we fully intend to perform... just not right now.

Oh, you're a poet? Yeah. You know, I really **should** *read more poetry.*

I know I'm always complaining about it. You're right, I **should** *look for a new job.*

Oh, you do? Funny, I was just thinking the other day, I really **should** *join a gym.*

No, not really. I know, she was always so sweet to me. Terrible what happened. I **should** *give her a call, say hello, see how she's doing.*

should = won't
(continued)

*That's so great of you. Yeah, in fact, I always think that's such a great idea and I totally **should** volunteer too.*

*I really shouldn't be going out tonight. I **should** just stay home, write that paper, be done with it.*

*I **should** just get over it. It happened. It's done. I shouldn't keep talking about it.... It's just that....*

*I can't believe it's been six hours. I **should** watch less television.*

*I keep saying it but, I really **should** get my financial situation straightened out.*

*Yeah, it's been out of control lately, but I know, I know. I **should** cut back on the drinking, eat better. I know.*

*Adoption? Wow. Really? Holy cow. That's.... Us? No, but, now that you mention it, we **should**. We really **should**. We **should** think about looking into it.*

think = know
The negation is an affirmation.

Close your eyes for a moment, concentrate, and please don't think about an elephant.

It's as good as telling you to, right?

I had a boss once who asked me, "Do you think I make you do more mundane work than I ask of Jim because you're a girl?"

Well, now I do. If the thought could enter his mind and bug him enough to want to check with me, it was probably true. A case of protesting too much.

I think imagination is rare, despite its alleged ubiquity. I don't have many fanciful worries. If I worry about your perception of me, it's probably because I did something to warrant it. Imagine if I said, "I don't want you to *think* I'm critical." Hasn't that ship sailed? I can't blame you for concluding it.

Most often the evasion *think = know* appears in the phrase: *I don't want you to think...*, which reveals more than intended, because that is in fact the case: I don't want you to think, leading as it would to an inevitable conclusion.

---

*We feel that allowing you to write self-evaluations involves every member of this organization in the decision-making process, and it gives management the essential feedback we need when determining such things as pay raises and promotions. We don't want our team to **think** every member doesn't have a voice.*

think = know
(continued)

*We always make it a point to involve our children in any discussion we have, about anything, politics even. We don't want them to **think** their opinions are less valid than ours.*

*We make sure to convey to our nanny that she's more than an employee, she's a member of the family. We don't want her to **think** she isn't on equal footing with us.*

*That wasn't me. I mean, it was me, but it wasn't me-me. I don't want you to **think** I drink too much and can't handle it.*

*We give each student a prize and praise their individual successes. We don't want young people to **think** they're in competition with one another.*

*It isn't easy for me to know that I did that. I mean, it's eating me up inside. I don't want you to **think** I'm the sort of person who can just do something like that.*

*Oh I'm just doing this for the money, just a few years, and then I'm out. I don't want you to **think** I'm like these other guys I work with, who like, believe in this shit.*

think = know
(continued)

*It's just been a tough week, all this shit going on at work. I don't usually do this. I don't want you to **think** I have such a short fuse.*

*I just wanted to explain and apologize for just up and leaving like that. I mean, I didn't want you to **think** I'm an asshole or something.*

unfortunately = um, fortunately

Obstacle is safeguard.

Being a perfectionist is sometimes a way to avoid doing something. It's not done, it's not quite right, I have to redo it—all of these delays postpone the possibility of failure.

It's easier to squander an opportunity than to try and fail. Sometimes we contrive reasons to disqualify ourselves from external tests and trials.

---

*I can't work on my résumé because **unfortunately**, my computer crashed. Otherwise, I would apply for that job and quit this dead-end pit.*

*Believe me, I would love to be a published writer. But **unfortunately** I don't have time to write anymore. Otherwise I would.*

*I want to stop worrying about my health so that I can enjoy life more, but **unfortunately**, there are so many problems at work right now, I can't be bothered.*

*I was so busy that **unfortunately**, I missed the deadline. I guess I can kiss that promotion goodbye. With the money this company pays, the extra responsibilities would have been worth it.*

unfortunately = um, fortunately
(continued)

*The baby came along, and now, **unfortunately**, I have no time anymore for painting. Otherwise, it would be my life.*

*I would be so much more focused at work but **unfortunately** I've been experiencing terrible insomnia lately. If only I could get a decent night's sleep.*

*We can't get married yet because **unfortunately** the band we had our heart set on is booked solid that week.*

*My wife and I were going to try to have a baby, but then I changed jobs, so **unfortunately**, right now's not the right time.*

*I wanted to apply for that job, but then that morning I thought I was coming down with something and **unfortunately** had to cancel my interview.*

*I would try for that job in a heartbeat, but **unfortunately**, I know someone who works there, and we do not get along at all.*

*Yeah, I got a full scholarship to attend that graduate program. It's the most competitive in the country, but **unfortunately**, my girlfriend doesn't want to relocate.*

unfortunately = um, fortunately
(continued)

*It was a great opportunity, and I'm sure I would have made the most of it, but my family comes first, so **unfortunately** I have to turn it down.*

*I have always regretted not going back to school. Maybe if I had, I would have left him and been more independent. But **unfortunately** opportunities didn't permit that.*

"We keep our insignificant blemishes so that we can blame them for our larger defects."

—Stephen Fry, *Moab is My Washpot*

I don't know what people did before the expression *well, duh*. If someone said, "I wonder if the politician is pandering just to get votes," did our forebears respond with, "Well, of course. That goes without saying"? How did that suffice for so long? The first person who spluttered *well, duh* must have felt many generations' worth of supreme satisfaction.

Likewise with the word *whatever*. Most popularly used as a concession to civility (see The Minced Oath *Whatever*), out of all the evasions, *whatever* has the most attitude. It's the Fonzie of the bunch, and since there's no denying that *whatever* is the verbal equivalent of an eye-roll, it isn't entirely an evasion.

But whatever. It qualifies as an evasion because there are many nuances to the word, none of which the speaker will do you the courtesy to tease out.

Whatever was popularized by the 1995 movie *Clueless*. The word has survived so long because of its versatility. It's petulance in a one-word sentence, sufficient unto itself, and best of all, *whatever* is one of the few evasions that acknowledges other evasions and can serve as a dismissive retort.

the apathetic *whatever*
Translation: Yeah so.

---

*She said I was insensitive and I was like, **whatever**.*

*Then he said I didn't have the dedication to the job that he wanted from his employees, and if I didn't do better on my next review, I might not get a raise, and I was all, **whatever**.*

*She wouldn't give me an extension on the paper. Wouldn't be fair to the others. **Whatever**.*

*Oh, I'm immature? **Whatever**.*

*She said I had an attitude problem, she didn't much appreciate how I spoke to her. **Whatever**.*

*My Mom went nuts. "How many times do I have to tell you? Answer me. How many times! I've said it over and over and over again, and do you listen? No. You don't listen. What do you have to say for yourself?" So I'm grounded again. **Whatever**.*

the pseudo-impartial *whatever*
Translation: Who am I to judge?

You know she was living in South Carolina for a while. Yeah, couple years ago, she met this guy, two months later, boom, they were married. Moved down there. They're divorced now. She has a kid. Quit school. **Whatever.**

He doesn't work. Lives at home. His parents take care of him. **Whatever.**

She's dating the boss. **Whatever.**

He belongs to one of those religious, spiritual groups, cults. No, not that one. Another one. **Whatever.**

Do you know that she's never tasted alcohol? Thinks it's wrong. **Whatever.**

the self-pitying *whatever*
Translation: Why do I always have to be the martyr?

---

*I don't know why it's called a group project because I did all the work, but **whatever**.*

*Really it wasn't much of a holiday since I was on my feet for three days preparing and then guess who cleaned up after everybody left, but **whatever**.*

*Never mind that I'm the one who came up with the idea in the first place, but **whatever**.*

*I helped her move. It ended up being a hell of a lot more than just a few boxes, like she said it was gonna be, and I totally threw out my back, and then she didn't even spring for pizza afterwards, but she's my best friend, so **whatever**.*

the slow thaw *whatever*
Translation: OK but I'm still gonna sulk.

"I feel so bad about this. What's say you let me take you out to dinner tomorrow night instead? Anyplace you want. What do you think about that? Wouldn't that be nice?"
   "Whatever."

"I'm so sorry Daddy had to miss your game. Let me try to make it up to you. Hey I know, let's go to the mall. I'll buy you those sneakers you wanted. What do you say? Doesn't that sound like a good idea?"
   "Whatever."

"This is the last time. I promise. Just give me another chance. Hey, I have an idea. Let's go on vacation. Don't you think we need a vacation? Get away from it all, a fresh start. Wouldn't you like that?"
   *"OK. I mean, **whatever**."*

the emotion kibosh *whatever*
Translation: Get over it.

And she was all, "You have to understand, I've been hurt before; I trusted you, and that's not an easy thing for me to do, considering my past, and you let me down, and you know it brought up all these issues for me," and I was just, **whatever***.*

It was awful. A forty-minute rant about how I'm a disappointment, and he always expected more from me, and I owe it to the family, and when he was my age, and what did I think I was gonna do with my life, what was I trying to say, and in his day..., and by now his face is turning blue and veins are sticking out of his neck and I was all, Dad, **whatever***. It's just a tattoo.*

At first he admitted it, and then he tried to make excuses. You know, it wasn't his fault, he grew up without a father, didn't really learn to trust, and he made one stupid mistake and already I'm breaking up with him, and it's gonna destroy him, and he doesn't wanna lose me, and at this point he's crying. **Whatever***.*

the evasion evader *whatever*

Translation: I'll see you an evasion and raise you one.

---

*She was all, "I love being with you, and I wouldn't trade our time together for anything in the world, but I just need this time alone." I just said, **whatever**.*

*He's so pathetic. He tried to be all, "I can't believe I did that to you. I feel terrible." But I was all, **whatever**.*

*She really spazzed out on me. "How could you do that? I mean, I went out my way to meet you there, and then you didn't show, and you didn't even call, and it was like...." So now she's mad at me. **Whatever**.*

*My boss stiffed us on bonuses. Gave us the song and dance about how he knew how hard we worked, and he wanted to do right by us, but his hands were tied. **Whatever**.*

the jealous *whatever*

Translation: Lucky stiff.

Turns out his uncle pulled a few strings and got him the job, but **whatever**.

Even though my SAT score's higher than hers, and I have all these like, extracurriculars. I don't know how she got accepted and I didn't but, **whatever**.

I waited on line all night for tickets. This one? He makes one phone call to his scalper friend, and he gets front-row seats. **Whatever**.

We've been working on this for two years. He waltzes in at the last minute and makes one suggestion and suddenly, he's the group leader. **Whatever**.

the minced oath *whatever*
Translation: Fuck you.

My Mom gave me the speech. You know, I'm very disappointed in you. Your father and I made it clear to you that you were to be home at 12. Do you know how worried we were? Do you? You have totally violated our trust. It'll take a lot to earn it back. Now go to your room and think about what you've done. I just said **whatever**.

*I tried to explain that my computer crashed but she's such a bitch, she just said she didn't believe me and that she was gonna give me an F. I said, "***Whatever***," and left her office.*

Big fat cop pulls me over and he's all, "Son, do you realize how fast you were going, I'm gonna have to give you a ticket," and I was just, **whatever**.

the faltering cliché *whatever*
Translation: Insert psychobabble here.

He has so much to work out on his own. I mean, it's like he can't love anybody else until he learns to love himself, or **whatever**.

I just want you to know that I'm there for you, if you need me. You can count on me for emotional support or **whatever**.

It would just be good for me to talk about it, to deal with it. For, I don't know. Closure or **whatever**.

I thought it was gonna help me work through my inner demons, or emotional wounds or **whatever**. *It didn't.*

You're supposed to get to this state of complete bliss, and your mind is supposed to be clear of any thought, and that's the ultimate peace, or **whatever**.

the bashful *whatever*
Translation: Oops, emotions. Sorry.

It was beautiful. I mean, I just looked up and there it was, the Sistine Chapel, and it was like so pure, and I know it sounds cheesy, but, it was like I was in the presence of, I don't know, God, or **whatever**.

That was such an amazing experience. At one point, everybody started singing along, and there was like this energy of, I don't know, total love, or **whatever**.

It was like we were on the same wavelength. We totally connected. It's like we're meant to be, like we're soul mates, or **whatever**.

the doubting thomas *whatever*
Translation: Liar, liar pants on fire.

And then he said he did try to call me, or he meant to, but he couldn't find my number and I was like, **whatever**.

It's over. She actually gave me the It's-not-you-it's-me line. **Whatever**.

What does he think, I'm a fool? He's not even a good liar. His story keeps changing. First he said he did say it, then he said he didn't, then he did say it but I took it the wrong way. **Whatever**.

the pleasantly surprised *you* = **I**

I disabuse you of my own
preconceptions.

A stereotype can be aired with impunity by being voiced and
then dismissed. "You hear that and you think..." can function
as an imperative, an instruction: "You, think!" It's a case of
leading the witness, your honor. The pleasantly surprised
speakers help you avoid the mistaken interpretation that they
themselves have made.

---

*He's so smart, **you** would think he's, you know,
unbearable to be around; but he's not at all
pretentious.*

*She's a classical musician, **you** would think she
only listens to classical shit but no, she knows
about new stuff too.*

*You hear she's a scientist, and **you** think, "Uh oh,"
but she's really interesting, fun to talk to.*

*He's a businessman, but **you** would be surprised;
he's creative, too. He paints.*

*He's a foreign teacher. He's from, I don't know,
something South American. **You** talk to him and
you realize he's really really articulate.*

the pleasantly surprised *you* = I
(continued)

*She's a model, but I talked to her a bit and **you**'d never guess it but she's not stupid.*

*He's really into reading, poetry and stuff, and **you** think he's gonna be all—but no, he's cool.*

*She's a housewife, and **you** think, "Oh, soap operas," but no; it's not like she doesn't do anything.*

***You** think they're gonna be all snooty when **you** hear they're really rich, but in fact they're friendly.*

the presumptuous *you* = I
Speak for yourself.

Using the word *you* instead of *I* is an unearned intimacy that fails to bring us closer together. Instead, it betrays that we don't distinguish between us.

---

*It's like when **you** swear you're gonna go to the gym and get totally healthy, and then like **you** don't.*

*You've been there, **you** say "I'll be good," and then **you** down a pint of ice cream anyway.*

*You know when **you** start a book and then **you** just give up and turn on the television?*

*You know when **you** have nothing planned for the evening and **you** call up anyone, old boyfriends, anything, just so that **you** can say that **you** did something that night?*

*You know when **you** have an affair and then feel really guilty about it afterwards?*

*It's like when **you** screw something up at work just to fuck over your boss.*

*You know when **you** have a bad day at work and then **you** take it out on the kids?*

*You know when **you** try to pick a fight with some-body just because?*

Maggie Balistreri edited *Popaganda: The Art and Subversion of Ron English*, and runs the language and poetry webzine *CafeMo.com*. She has written about language for numerous publications, including *Vocabula.com, LaPetiteZine, thescreamonline.com*, and *Slope*. Born in Brooklyn, she works in the New York publishing industry as a copy editor, and is also a rock climber, a dirt-bike racer, and a biography embellisher.

acknowledgments

For your unremitting excellence, thank you to Franco and Gina Balistreri, Carol and Johnny Balistreri, Miss Jenny Benka (T.P.), Donna Christensen, Christi DiGangi, Dennis Loy Johnson and Valerie Merians, Gene Bryan Johnson, Margarita at St. Marks Bookshop, Krista Pfeiffer, Larry and Pat Ronaldson.